ZELMA'S APHORISMS OLD SCHOOL WISDOM, INSTRUCTIVE, INSPIRATIONAL, HILARIOUS, TO OUTRAGEOUS

Zelma's Aphorisms Old School Wisdom, Instructive, Inspirational, Hilarious, to Outrageous

Maurice W. Dorsey

Rev. date: 08/30/2022

To order additional copies of this book, contact:
Xlibris
844-714-8691
www.Xlibris.com
Orders@Xlibris.com
840221

CONTENTS

In loving memory of my mother, Zelma Virginia Curry-Dorsey

Acknowledgments

Thanks to family, colleagues, and friends who have advised, guided, recommended, hosted a book signing, purchased one or more of my three books, or simply applauded my writing journey. There were some challenging times during this development and writing process. These individuals were of great comfort and pushed me to the finish line. They are listed alphabetically.

Ray Ali, EdD
Michele Ali, Esq.
Lynn Andrews, Esq.
Mr. Tony Angelini
Mr. Leroy Bailey
Ms. Martha J. Bridgeforth
Mr. Dominique Brightmon
Ms. Francesca Britton
Barry S. Brown, PhD
Ms. Trena Taylor-Brown
Mr. Ernest Brooks
Ms. Joyce Brooks
Cheri Bridgeforth Castillo, PhD
Julio Castillo, JD
Mrs. Debbie Cavett
Virginia Wenger Cobb, PhD
Mr. and Mrs. Brian A. Dorsey and Sons
Cheryl L. Dorsey, MD
Major and Mrs. Eric L. Dorsey and Son

Ms. Margaret Jane Russell Hill Dorsey
Mr. and Mrs. Stephen Mark Dorsey
Mrs. Zelma V. Dorsey
Thomas Eagle, PhD
Mr. Richard Brent Elrod
Mr. Michael Gold
Michael Loren Harris, PhD
Ms. Gwendolyn Jackson
Judge Neal M. Janey, Esq.
Bernie Jones, Esq.
James Jones, Esq.
Mrs. Gracie Joy
Mr. Scott Lubbock
Barbara Maidment, EdD
Mr. John Thomas Martin
Frederic Breed Mayo, PhD, MBA
Mr. Glenn Royce Nixon
Ms. Michele Noel
Anna Palmisano, PhD
Ms. Anna De Cheke Qualls
Mr. Tom Tate
Mr. Julio Tumbaco
Gladys Gary Vaughn, PhD
Mr. Henry Westray
James B. Wolcott, MD
Mr. William Wood
Mr. Earl Wynn
Mr. Silas R. Young

Introduction

My mother was the firstborn to a stable mother and father. She was faced with hardship at a very early age with the death of her mother, who died when my mother was eight years old. My mother had to assume the roles of her mother in raising herself and two other children. In addition, she played the role of a surrogate wife to her father, who was described as a lazy man. These very early adult responsibilities cheated my mother out of most of her childhood. She also attended school each weekday and church on Sunday; thus, there was little time for play.

She eventually married, gave birth to three children, and had to start child rearing again, building a career and, at the end of her life, possessing and enjoying many aspects of life that were denied her in childhood.

Zelma's Aphorisms, Old-School Wisdom, Instructive, Inspirational, Hilarious to Outrageous is a compilation of the many old sayings she used to raise her younger sister and brother, as well as her own three children. It was often just quick wit that she had picked up from her father and older adult mothers who helped guide her in the role of raising children and being married to a man.

The essence of my mother's aphorisms are in my head from a lifetime of good memories. My mother talked to me from birth to first grade, first grade through high school, and then through telephone conversations while I was away in college. We discuss all the growing pains of young adulthood and self-sufficiency. We talked until her final days. It is needless to say we were close. We had our ups and downs, but she was in my corner my entire life. Oftentimes, when I reflected back, I didn't know how deeply my mother loved me.

We spoke of the value of education, the difficulties of puberty, the consequences of teen sexuality, saving money for a rainy day, straight and gay relationships, career responsibilities and the frustrations of the daily grind, and everything in between. Her aphorisms were instructive for me, but sometimes difficult to understand as a child and teenager. I really had to give some of them some thought before I could procure the essence of her points. My mother could be loud and sometimes harsh in expressing her teachings. But she wanted me to understand in a powerful way what she was saying and that she didn't have much time in her day to pamper you. You had to get her message right then and there. Sometimes it was a struggle, and sometimes she was as hilarious in the manner in which she spoke.

We also discussed her short life with her mother; living with her lazy, overbearing older father; raising her younger sister and brother; being raised in the Methodist Church; living in poverty for many years during the Great Depression; and her exposure to Washington, DC, as a colored girl. This all led up to her wit, quick retorts, and immediate response and reflex to a life she did not choose.

CHRONOLOGY

Birth of William Henry Curry Sr. (her father, a.k.a. Papa), Washington, DC, May 26, 1877.

Birth of Mary (Mae) Letcher Williams (her mother), Staunton, Virginia, March, 26, 1895.

Birth of Zelma Virginia Curry, Washington, DC, September 2, 1919.

Birth of Agnes Elizabeth Curry (her sister), Washington, DC, February 20, 1921.

Birth of William Henry Curry Jr. (her brother), Washington, DC, July 3, 1923.

Attended B. K. Bruce Elementary School, Washington, DC, 1925.

Attended Lucretia Mott Elementary School, Washington, DC, 1925–1930.

Death of Mary (Mae) Letcher Curry, Washington, DC, November 16, 1927.

Attended Burrville Elementary School, Washington, DC, 1926–1927.

Attended Garnett Patterson Junior High School, Washington, DC, 1927–1933.

Attended Dunbar Senior High School, Washington, DC, 1933-1936.

Graduated Frederick Douglass High School, Evening School, Baltimore, Maryland, 1936–1937.

Employed Reverend and Mrs. Robert Lewis, Washington, DC, 1936–1938.

Employed Reliable Employment Agency, Baltimore, Maryland, 1938–1939

Employed Pariser Bakery, Baltimore, MD, 1939–1940.

Marriage to James Roswell Dorsey Sr., Baltimore, Maryland, November 18, 1939.

Birth of James Roswell Dorsey, Jr., Baltimore, Maryland, June 20, 1940.

Birth of Margaret Elizabeth Dorsey, Baltimore, Maryland, September 16, 1941.

Catholic Baptism, St. Pius Church, Baltimore, Maryland, 1942.

Employed Harford County Public Schools, Edgewood, Maryland, 1943–1945.

Employed Army-Air Force Exchange, Edgewood Arsenal, Maryland, 1945–1948.

Birth of Maurice Wayne Dorsey, Baltimore, Maryland, May 10, 1947.

Employed United States Army, Edgewood Arsenal, Maryland, 1952–1979.

Death of William H. Curry Sr., Washington, DC, September 5, 1955.

Department of the Army, Ten-Year Certificate of Service, September 30, 1963.

Drexel University, Reference Librarian Training, Aberdeen Proving Ground, Maryland, April 1, 1963.

Federal Librarians Orientation and Workshop, Library of Congress, Washington, DC, May 24, 1966.

Cataloging and Classification Training, Drexel University, Aberdeen Proving Ground, Maryland, 1956–1966.

Reference Materials Course, Drexel University, Aberdeen, Maryland, April to June, 1966.

Certificate of Proficiency, Operations of MT/ST Selectric Typewriter, International Business Machines (IBM), July 15, 1966.

Member of the Ames United Methodist Church, Bel Air, Maryland, July 1971.

Harford Community College, Chemistry, Man, and Society, Bel Air, Maryland, June, 1974.

Outstanding Performance as Library Technician, Technical Information Branch, Development Support, Aberdeen Proving Ground, Maryland, September 12, 1977.

Meets Oprah Winfrey, Frey Club, Aberdeen, Maryland, June 17, 1979.

Certificate of Recognition for accumulation of one thousand hours of sick leave (ten years of never missing a day of work due to illness), United States Army Material Development and Readiness Command, Aberdeen Proving Ground, Maryland, September 12, 1979.

James Roswell Dorsey Sr. dies, Baltimore, Maryland, December 2, 2000.

Certificate of appreciation for faithful membership and supporter of Ames

United Methodist Church, Harford County Office of the County
Executive, Bel Air, Maryland, April 28, 2001.

National Campaign of Tolerance, authorized the name of Zelma V. Dorsey
be added to the Wall of Tolerance, signed by Rosa Parks and Morris
Dees, co-chairs, February 17, 2003.

CHAPTER ONE

Era of Zelma's Birth

Her children arise up, and call her blessed;
her husband also, and he praiseth her.
—Proverbs 31:28

My mother was born in Washington, DC, with Staunton, Virginia, roots from her mother's side of the family. My mother was a southern lady at her roots. She was African American, legitimate, and born free. She was born in 1919, a transformative year for the United States. There were race riots, women were fighting for the right to vote, communism was infiltrating the country, and labor strikes were taking place all over the country. The beginning of prohibition and the Civil Rights Movement were also taking place.

Earlier in the 1900s, President Theodore Roosevelt invited Booker T. Washington to the White House to dine for dinner in 1901. Booker T. Washington was the first African American to be invited to the White House to dine with a United States president. Public anger and excitement resulted from this casual presidential invitation from conflicting factions.

In April of 1903, W. E. B. Du Bois, author of *The Souls of Black Folk* was published. In his book, Du Bois rejected Booker T. Washington's gradualism approach to race relationships in America and called for agitation on behalf of African American Rights.

In 1904, Mary McLeod Bethune, an African American educator,

founded the Bethune-Cookman College located in Daytona Beach, Florida.

Thurgood Marshall was born in 1908. He was the attorney for the National Association for the Advancement of Colored People (NAACP) in the landmark *Brown v. Board of Education,* in which the Supreme Court found segregated schools to be inherently unequal. Later, he was appointed the first African American to the Supreme Court of the United States.

The City Council of Baltimore approved the first city ordinance designating boundaries for black and white neighborhoods in December 1910. Similar ordinances creating segregated neighborhoods occurred in the states of Texas, North Carolina, Kentucky, Virginia, Oklahoma, and Missouri.

President Woodrow Wilson (Democrat) was elected president in 1912. My mother's aunt, Louise Dunmore, was one of the White House cooks under his administration. He presented her with a set of China when he exited the White House. My mother and her sister, Agnes, reported they made mud cakes on with the China, never knowing, as children, their value. One plate remains. Being a White House cook was a status position for an African American at the time. One year later, President Wilson ushered in government-wide segregation of the workplace, restrooms, and lunchrooms.

The United States entered World War I in 1917. Three hundred seventy African Americans were in military service, and more than half were in the French war zone.

Lynching took place throughout the decade my mother was born, and race riots were gaining momentum. This is the setting of my mother's birth.

* * *

The inspiration and structure of *Zelma's Aphorisms, Old-School Wisdom* comes from the *Book of Proverbs.* Proverbs is the book of wisdom for living. Its teachings include instruction on folly, sin, goodness, wealth, poverty, the tongue, pride, humility, justice, vengeance, strife, gluttony, love, lust, laziness, friends, family, life, and death. Almost every facet of human relationships is mentioned. These teachings are applicable to all men everywhere.

My mother was born and raised in the Ebenezer United Methodist Church at Third and D Street Southeast Washington, DC. Although she attended church on a regular basis throughout her life, she filtered the teachings of the church and balanced the teachings with her life experience and common sense. That being said, she did not believe in every interpretation of the Bible. My mother's thinking matured to this level after the death of her mother. At the age of eight years old, my mother, the oldest of three children, was made to assume the female roles of the Curry household. This included caring for her father and two younger siblings. My mother was God-fearing, a believer in a supreme being, but at this age and level of responsibility, she had to grow up fast, missing out on most of her childhood.

Proverbs goes back in written form to about 2700 BC in Egypt. Proverbs 31:10–31 describes the function of the capable wife. In formatting *Zelma's Aphorisms*, I have selected a verse from Proverbs 31: 10–31 to introduce each chapter. These verses best describe my mother from my sixty-seven years with her, and although deceased now, my memories of her are powerfully alive.

I saw my mother as my mother and my very best friend. I happened to say this to her once. She replied very sharply, "I am your mother, not your friend." Nevertheless, in my heart she was my best friend too.

I am by no means a theologian, nor was my mother; however, the specific verse 31:28, "Her children arise up, and call her blessed; her husband also, and he praiseth her," me, as author, arise and call her blessed. Her teachings of wisdom were not as eloquent as the writers of Proverbs. My mother's wisdom was often raw, direct, and to the point. She had the ability to quickly set a man, woman, or child straight with her words. She had strong defense mechanisms for her survival in which she learned from her very difficult childhood. At times I would ask my mother what she meant by her sayings, and she would say, "Well, if you give it some thought, you will understand, and that I get my point across, and if that doesn't work, then just keep living. You will eventually understand." Just Keep Living was her mantra.

"Just keep living!"

In my mind, my mother was a virtuous woman. She performed many great deeds and survived many of her contemporaries, famous and not so famous, in living what I thought was a successful life. She lived for ninety-five years through good and bad circumstances.

CHAPTER TWO

Early Years

Many daughters have done virtuously,
but thou excellest them all.
—Proverbs 31:29

Zelma's Aphorisms, Old-School Wisdom begins in Washington, DC, with her father, William Henry Curry.

My grandfather was born in Washington, DC, in 1877. He was born free, colored; he was a self-employed laborer. He was an only child, and according to my mother, he was spoiled, had average intelligence but a ton of common sense, and took charge of everything he could. He was a church-going Methodist and a member of the Masonic Order of Masons. As a single man, he was considered worldly and consorted with many women. He was called a talking sensation. He could hold a small group captive with his loquacious conversation, jovial personality. He learned to maneuver his way into the world of finesse.

He married Mary Letcher Williams; they called her Mae. She was from Staunton, Virginia. She was born into a prominent Negro family. She was eighteen years younger than her husband. She was soft and kind. Her life's desire was to become a missionary for her church. It was said that my grandfather talked her into marriage. He moved her from Staunton, Virginia, to Washington, DC, after they married. She worked as a cook, and he continued his self-employment as a handyman/laborer. She was dominated by her controlling husband.

They had three children: Zelma, Agnes, and William Jr., whom they called Billy. Zelma was the female version of her father. Agnes was a delicate child like her mother. Billy was his mother's pride and joy, but different. William was habitually cruel to Billy. He would force Billy to put on one of the girls' dresses and make him stand in the living room window so that all the children in the neighbor would laugh at him as punishment for having poor grades in school. All three children were born at Columbia Women's Hospital. The children were required to attend church every Sunday and attend school on weekdays. William preached to his children: "I am going to give you your health and strength and a chance to make it in the world" Beyond this, he felt he had met his obligation as a father.

My grandfather had a reputation for standing up to white men that he worked for or came in contact with. He would say boisterously, "Now, don't you 'Uncle Tom' me! I am not your uncle Tom. My name is William H. Curry, and I wish to be addressed as such!" Often, this response would lead to a loss of job opportunities. White men often could not tolerate my grandfather's threatening attitude, nor did my grandfather like being disrespected. He stood up for himself but paid a high price. He would lose jobs, thus couldn't pay his rent, and would need to relocate his family to different residences. The children had changed schools as a result of my grandfather's need to be respected. The family was rootless.

He worked for a black man named Mr. Peacock, who refused to pay him for a job he completed. He would argue with the man eye-to-eye and toe-to-toe until he got his money. After my grandfather was fully paid for his services and pocketed the money, he would retort, "You are a nasty man, and you have a nasty name!"

To his children and grandchildren, my grandfather well-ordered his children to speak up. He would say to them, as brash as he could, "Speak up! Don't walk around here acting like you don't have a brain in your head! Speak up!"

He also ordered, his children to call him sir. "It is not yes or no! It is 'yes, sir!' You speak to me 'yes, sir!' or 'no, sir!' And you address an elder with a handle to his or her name, mister or missus! You don't go around here calling an adult by their first name! It is disrespectful!"

He voiced in softer tones to each of his children, "Success is having the title to a car and a deed to a house! Then you can call yourself a success! Until then, you don't own a tinker's damn!"

William Henry put all his children out to work after his wife died and the Great Depression hit the nation. This was before child labor laws were implemented and enforced. He would say to them, "Get out of bed before the sun bakes wheat cakes on your backsides!" His children worked before and after school. When payday arrived, he precisely took all their earning to run the household. Times were tough. The children were not happy with him taking all their money and leaving none for them. The girls were missing many of the feminine niceties that young girls with mothers enjoyed. They were poor and looked poor. All three children were ridiculed in school each day for their deprived dress and grooming.

He would chastise his children after taking all their money, saying, "When you go out on your own to earn money for yourself, 'if you make a nickel, save a cent'!" This translated to saving 20 percent and not 10 percent as was commonly recommended. He would also say, "Hold on to a dollar until it screams out 'I am your friend!'" My grandfather was a firm advocate of "God bless the child who has his own"!

My mother revered her father's strength and take-charge nature. She, however, was the child who was a victim of his harshness when she disobeyed. She, like her father, spoke up and defended herself, unlike her mother and sister. She belittled her mother's softness. She disliked the verbal abuses her mother endured from her father. Her mother was rural and not accustomed to urban living. She was timid and shy. She cried each time her husband left home at night to go attend Masonic meetings, leaving her alone with three children. Her father's solution to the problem was to purchase a German shepherd to protect his family, rather than stay at home with his wife and children and skip the Masonic meetings. If my mother disagreed, she said as much and was whipped and punished for doing what he taught her to do. "Speak up!" My grandfather's teachings did not apply to him, and especially not to his children and daughter too.

William Henry Curry was a case. He was a lifelong resident of Washington, DC, and died September 5, 1955 (Labor Day) of heart disease at the age of seventy-eight. His wife, Mary Letcher Curry, died prematurely on November 16, 1927. Zelma was eight years old.

After Mae died, this is where my mother's wisdom was jettisoned. The household changed, and she became fully responsible for the female functions of running the home. This included washing and ironing clothes, cooking, feeding her siblings, and cleaning the house. Her father made her learn how to change the tires on his Model T car; he laughed and snickered as he peeped through the curtains, watching his daughter change the tires on his car.

At Zelma's birth, the family lived at 929 Third Street SE, Washington, DC. She attended Lucretia Mott Elementary School from 1925 to 1930.

The family later moved to Northeast Washington and resided at 245 Eastern Avenue from 1926 to 1929. This was considered a step up in Washington, DC, housing for a Negro family. It was at this location that Mae took to her bed with illness and later passed away. Times were hard; she had given birth to three children in a short period of time. The Great Depression hit the nation along with people everywhere who were losing all they had. The cause of Mae's death was never determined; however, it was assumed it was from the stress of relocation from her home state of Virginia, having children, being afraid of the city, and most of all, marrying a less-than-attentive husband. Zelma attended Burrville Elementary School in 1926–1927. Somewhere in the mayhem, she temporarily resided at 245 Iowa Avenue and attended Bruce Elementary School.

The family moved again to 1007 Monroe Street NW and resided here from 1929 to 1936. Zelma attended Garnett Patterson from 1930 to 1933. She was in the academic program.

The family moved again to Forty-Ninth Street NE from 1936 to 1937. Zelma attended Dunbar Senior High School from 1933 to 1936 and attended and graduated night school from the Douglas High School in Baltimore, Maryland, in 1938–1939.

While completing her education, she was employed by Reverend and Mrs. Robert Lewis at Lowell Street NW in 1936–1938. It was during the summer of 1938 that she moved to Baltimore to get away from her father. She lived with her father's adoptive sister—she called her Aunt Willie—in 1316 Division Street. Her younger sister had left home a few years ahead of Zelma and lived with this same aunt at the same address.

Her sister married, but the marriage ended in an unhappy divorce. Her sister was so distraught she was placed in a state hospital until she could take care of her child. Zelma, here again, was a dutiful sister and traveled long distances to visit her ailing sister regularly.

Zelma was now in her midthirties. She and James both secured government jobs and were slowly getting ahead. Her father telling her, as a child, that success equaled having a title to a car and a deed to a house echoed. She did not have that at this point, but she was driven to be a success.

This was a tumultuous existence for any child. Zelma survived.

CHAPTER THREE

Zelma's Aphorisms

She openeth her mouth with wisdom; and
in her tongue is the law of kindness.
—Proverbs 31:26

Note: All italics are Zelma's emphasis on words as she made her pronouncements.

A Good Day
"I'm doing okay today, *I am up on all fours*!"

A Good Surprise
"*Well, for the love of God*!"

A Lull in Communications
"*No news* is good news!"

A Mother's Life
"When children are young they are *on your feet*, when they get old they are *on your heart*, you never get finished with them!"

A Once Spry Person Who Has Gotten Old
"Now, *they are all old and doedy!*"

A Parent's Gift
"I am giving you your health and strength, *and a chance* to make it in the world!"

A Person Who Talks Too Much
"*Telegraph, telephone and tell* (name)!"

Absolutely No
"*Not living!*"

Adults and Children with a Whiny Voice
"Learn to speak up! *Don't act like you don't have a tongue in your head,* speak up!"

Advancing Age
"My life is *ebbing away!*"

Advice to Recalcitrant Children
"If you want to do it your way, *suit yourself,* yes, go right ahead. I have been on this earth longer than you, and I am giving you the right answer. I am trying to help you, not hurt you, so if you decide to do it your way, *don't come crying to me and expecting me to nurse your wounds when you fall!*"

Note: After you made a poor decision, she would watch you jump off a cliff. She was guiltless. She valued her life experiences and shared them. If her children and others were *hell-bent* on doing the wrong thing, she let them because then she felt she had discharged her duties as a mother/friend.

After a Sleepless Night
"I feel like a *zombie!*"

After Her Death
"I will be *pushing up* daisies!"

Aging
"All I can say is, *don't get old!*"

All You Can Expect
"*That's just* par for the course!"

Alternate Plan
"You have to *make shift*, to make it work!"

An Aging Face
"*Time is taking its toll*!"

Angry
"So now, *you got your behinds up on your back*!"

Annoying Child
"You are becoming a *plumb nuisance*!"

Acquaintances
"*Familiarity breeds contempt*! Don't tell *all* your business!"

Are You Crazy?
"I know, you must be *sick*!"

Arguing Person
"You are acting *pug ugly*!"

Asking for Too Much
"*You want too much sugar for a cent*!"

Attacked by Someone
"*Go to* war!"

Attitude toward Housework
"You do some *and leave some*!"

Bad Choice
"That will learn you, *durn* [darn] *you*!"

Bad Choice, When Correctly Advised
"*Well, that's your little red wagon*!"

Bagging Groceries Yourself
"These stores are always talking about providing service. *There is no service, you have to do everything your damn self!*"

Balancing Your Money
"Spend some, and *save* some!"

Barber Shop
Ms. Zelma how you doing? "Everybody, I can, *and fools twice!*"

Bathing
"*You smell tired* and musty, go take a bath!"

Be Careful
"You have to *gauge* the situation!"

Be Kind
"Because you don't know whose ass you are going to have kiss before you leave this earth!"

Be Strong
"*Grit your teeth and ride it out!*"

Beaming
"You are *grinning from ear to ear,* like a Cheshire cat"

Beggars and Leeches
"No news, is good news!"

Being a Mother Disappointed
"Mothers are *sorry* creatures!"

Being Grateful
"You are begging for more shoes when there are *some people who would be happy to have your feet!*"

Being Nice to Yourself

"You have to be able to *treat yourself sometimes*, otherwise, *what is the point of living?*"

Being Taken Advantage
"Man, *they got you coming and going!*"

Big Feet
"You have a good *understanding.*"

Bitch
"Son of a *bench hook!*"

Body Odor
"You smell tired!"

Boys and Men Wearing Underwear in the Kitchen
"Puts some clothes on boy, *I don't want your stuff swinging around my food!*"

Braggers
"Who are you, *the Great* I am?"

Breathing through Your Mouth
"*Close your mouth, a fly may fly in it!*"

Burnt or Overcooked Food
"Well, eat it anyway, *it makes you look pretty!*"

Business before Pleasure
"Always, *take care of business first!*"

Busy
"*I got roads to go down!*"

By Any Means
"*By hook or by crook!*"

Can't Pay Your Bills
"Well, *I guess you have to go begging!*"

Can't Solve an Easy Problem
"*That's just tough!*"

Can't Solve *This* Problem
"*Well, you had better go and have a chat with your Chaplin!*"

Catching Up or Trying to Get Ahead
"Every time I take one step forward, *something crops up*, and then I have to take two steps backward"

Cheap Bread
"*This stuff* taste like chewing gum!"

Cheap Labor
"Slipshod work, *you get what you pay for!*"

Cheap Person
"You should have *the first dollar* you ever made!"

Cheapest Meat
"*This is the last piece of meat jumping across the fence!*"

Child Repeatedly Asking for Money
"*What do you think? Money grows on trees.*"

Child Running Away from Home
"It is okay with me, but when you do, *you leave everything in here* [the house] *that I brought for you!*"

Child That Threatens to Run Away from Home
"Well, *I don't have you locked up in here*, if you can do better, the door is unlocked, and *there will be one less mouth here to feed!*"

Child That Wants to be Babied
"*Musha's* little baby!"

Children Addressing an Adult
"You don't go around here addressing an adult by their first name, you say 'mister' or 'missus.' *You put a handle on their name.*"

Children around Adult Conversations
"Children are to be seen and not heard!"

Children Responding to an Adult
"You respond to adults by saying 'yes, sir,' or 'no, sir,' 'yes, ma'am' or 'no, ma'am', *and don't say 'huh,' people will think you don't have any sense!*"

Clean
"It's *spanking* clean!"

Clean House Standard
"I like my house clean, but *I don't give a hoot nor a toot* if it is untidy!"

Close Haircut
"You ain't got nothing up there (on your head) *but some peach fuzz!*"

Common Cold Advice
"Well, *you feed a cold*, and starve a fever!"

Comparisons
"*You can't miss what you can't measure!*"

Complaint about Her Cooking
"*Just eat it!*"

Confidence
"*When I was ten, people thought I was thirty-five* because I had so much wisdom!"
Note: After her mother's death, she had to learn all the mother roles starting at eight years old, thus she learned a lot from older neighboring ladies.

Conversation with Women
"Oh! We are just sitting here chin-chitting!"

Cooking in a Hurry
Can I help you? "No, just get out of the kitchen and *let me throw this stuff together.*"

Credit Card Overspending
"Just wait until the bill comes in, you won't be so happy then!"

Crying Child
"*The poor little fellow!*"

Customer Service
"There is no such thing as customer service these days. *You have to pump your own gas, bring your own bags and bag your own food, and if you call the merchant, they tell you to go to www!* There is no such thing as customer service anymore, *you have to do everything your damn self!*"

Day before Payday
"*We sliding in here on a wing and a pray!* Yes, sir, counting pennies and praying!"

Death, Premature
"*Die young and make pretty corps!*"

Debt
"*You are not saving money as long as you owe somebody!*"

Deceased Husband
"Well, when you have been married to a man for over sixty years, some days you are glad they are gone!"

Decorating
"Furniture and accessories need to go along with *the motif* of the room."

Delicacies
"Bacon is a delicacy, *you don't make a meal of it.*"

Departures
"Okay, everybody! *I am getting ready to do the paper doll and cut out!*"

Dinah Washington Singing "Great God Almighty, You Are Nobody until Somebody Loves You"
"Now, she did not need to say all of that!"
Note: She liked Dinah Washington's songs; however, she did not think that "Great God Almighty" should be associated and sung in a bar or where alcohol was being served.

Desperate to Have Someone
"They have latched on to . . ."

Disapproval
"I am going to lay you among the sweet peas!"

Disciplining Youth
"Spare the rod and spoil the child!"

Displeased
"Well, it's a tough tidy, but it's got to be sucked!"

Displeasure with Housework
"Housework *is for the birds!"*

Disrespect
"I will kill any one of my children who disrespects me!"
Note: I don't know, but I was not going to test her; she had a gun.

Do Not Repeat Bad Behavior
"As long as you have a hole in your backside, I don't ever want to see or hear you do that again!"

Don't Accept All Invitations
"Afterward, *you feel obliged to return the invitation, and in some instances, you don't want to.* So if you don't accept the invitation in the first place, then you don't feel obligated to return the favor!"

Don't Be a Fool
"Now don't go around here *letting people talk holes in your head!"*

Don't Be Taken Advantage On
"Don't accept any *wooden nickels!*"

Don't Even Think It
"Perish the thought!"

Don't Force a Child to Eat
"Just let it sit there [on the table], *when they get hungry they will eat it!*"
Note: My mother knew hunger; when you are truly hungry, you will eat anything.

Don't Get into Trouble
"Now don't go out here and *get yourself all hemming up* into something you can't get yourself out of!"

Don't Loan Money
"Because when push comes to shove, they come up with some lame excuse for why they can't pay you back. *If you want them to have it, then just give it to them, and all call it even Steven!*"

Don't Take Advantage of Good People
"*You don't ride a good horse to death!*"

Don't Worry about Anything Too Long
"One hundred years from now, *it won't make any difference!*"

Door Partially Open
"Just *crack* the door!"

Double No
"One thing is for certain, and *two things are for sure!*"

Doubtful
"I have a *sneaking suspicion!*"

Dream Big
"*If you settle in life for a dime, then a dime is all you will get!*"

Dreamers
"Well, *wonders never cease!*"

Dress or Pants Stuck in Your Butt
"You are *cutting butter!*"
Note: Just imagine!

Dressed Well and Prosperous-Looking Man
"Hey, Ace! *Can you loan me a couple of dollars?*"

Dressy
"Sunday-*go-to-meeting clothes.*"

Dressy Dressed
"Well, let me go and put on my *glad rags!*"

Drinking Slow
"Your father is over there *nursing that gin!*"

Drunk Woman Driver
"*She wrapped that car around a pole.*"

Dumb and Dumber
"Well, now that is a situation of *the blind leading the blind!*

Dysfunctional Person
"Well, they are just *warped!*"

Eating Too Fast
"Why are you 'guzz-ing' [guzzling] down your food like that?"

Enduring Circumstances without Feeling
"I am just *going through the motions!*"

Less energetic
"*My get-up and go, just got-up and went!*"

Enough Sex Life
"I am throwing in the towel!"

Entertainment
"When visitors come to your home, *you must serve a collation"*

Enthusiastic
"Yeah! They are all *hepped up!"*

Excuses
"You have more excuses *than Carter has little liver pills!"*

Excuses
"Now, here, you come *up in here* with some song and dance about why you can't get the job done!"

Excitable
"You are working yourself up into a lather!"

Explain Yourself
"What have you done now?"

Expressionless
"Well, don't sit there *looking blank!"*

Extra Body Weight
"Well, you need to have a few extra pounds so that when you get sick *your body has something extra to draw upon!"*

Fast
"You are quicker than *Grant going through Richmond!"*

Fatigue
"My mind is willing, but *my body is not able!"*

Feeling Defeated
"I lay me down and bleed awhile, and get up and start all over again!"

Feeling Married for Too Long
"I am just *serving time!*"

Feelings of Guilt
"Your conscious will whip the hell out of you."

Flaming Hot Mother
"I work every day. I shop for the food, I pay for the food, I place it in the car, I bring it in the house, I cook it, and *now I have to beg you children to come to the table and eat it!*"
Note: Her teenagers are a challenge.

Flirtation, Men
"If you can keep the thought out of your head, I can keep the taste out of your mouth."

Fool
"The party is all over, your friends are gone, and you have *spent up all your money*, now you are broke. Now what are you going to do?"
Note: Some people don't have common sense.

Foolish Behavior
"Don't start acting like a clown, like you are down on a plantation somewhere and don't have any sense!"

Forcing the Point
"I don't want it shoved down my throat, if you don't agree, you don't agree, *just agree to disagree!*"

Friends
"Stick with the bridge that takes you safely across."

Frisky Man
"Man, *go shake your business!*"

Frowning Face
"Why do you have your face *all knotted up?*"

Farther Down the Road
"I will be pushing up daisies when that happens!"

Generous Gift
"Gee! This is a boat load!"
Note: She appreciated the gifts.

Get Out of the Way
"Ugger, ugger, out of the way!"
Note: *Ugger* was the sound of the horn on the old Model T Ford.

Gifts
"It's the thought that counts!"

Giving and Receiving
"Well, a dog will take a bone!"

Giving Credit Where Credit Is Due
"Well, you have to *give a dog his dues!"*

Going Dutch Treat
"That's for the younger women. In my generation, the men treated women, plus when a woman gets older, she needs her money to look presentable, otherwise the men are looking at some younger women!"

Goodbye
"Well, I am leaving now, but *like Douglas MacArthur, I shall return!"*

Good Idea
"Well, that *sounds like a winner!"*

Good Job
"Yeah, man, you are *on the ball!"*

Good Job, Exceptional Performance
"You will have stars in your crown."

Good Night to the Breastfeeding Baby
"Good night, *and nurse!*"

Good Sleep
"*If God made anything better than sleep, he kept it for himself.*"

Gossip
"A dog that brings a bone will take a bone!"

Grateful Mother
"When *you don't have to take cookies to your children in jail!*"

Greeting a Man
"How are you doing, Ace?"

Greeting a Woman
"How are you doing, chickadee?"

Grooming for Girls
"Girls must shave their underarms and sit in a tub of water!"

Group of Old People
"*The poor old souls, they are feeble now*, I feel sorry for them!"

Guest Planned to Arriving
"Well, I guess I need to get this house in *some semblance of order!*"

Habits of Other People Can Be Annoying
"It's okay to be yourself, but *I don't want a steady diet of it!*"

Half-Hearted
"They ain't doing nothing but making some *feeble attempt!*"

Happiness
"Happiness is *fleeting* in this world, you have a few moments here and there!"

Hardheaded
"You are *thickheaded!*"

Hardheadedness
"Okay, your hard head is going to *make for a soft behind*!"

Health and Aging
"Keep living, it gets worse!"

Honestly
"Well, I swear *to my rest*!"

Hostility
"*You are just holding animosity*!"

Hot
"It is as hot as *Hades*!"

Hot Temperature Outside
"It is a *scorcher* out there!"

Houseguest
"Clean up after they leave, not before they come. *You are just making extra work for yourself*!"

Housecleaning
"I've got to *whip this house into shape*!"

Housework Again
"Housework is *such a vicious cycle*!"

How a Woman Should Judge a Man
"*Check out his shoes and his shirt collar*, if his shoes and collar are dirty, he is no good!"

How Much Did That Cost
"*How much did they stick you for that*?"

Human Characteristics
"How did you get so *knock-kneed*?"

Hunger
"*My stomach thinks my throat was cut*, I am so hungry!"

Hurt Feelings
"Well then, *you just put your tail between your legs and go on about your business!*"

Husband Needs New Underwear
"Buy yourself some underwear, *the ones you have on look like a bowl of Yaka Mein!*"

I Don't Care
"I don't give a *tinker's damn!*"

Impossible
"Well, *you can't draw blood out of a beet!*"
Note: Why insist on something that won't work?

I Intended
"*The road to hell* is paved with people with good intentions!"

In a Big Hurry
"Okay, now, let's *make it snappy!*"

Incontinent
"Now, just look at yourself, you just 'shistyed' all over yourself!"

Infidelity
"*What's new?*" "I am not letting some other women hang curtains up in my house further, I can look up longer than a man can look down! They get old and broken down, and *they eventually have to come in*, then, they expect you to take care of them in their dotage."
Note: Now, isn't this a fine "how do you do."

Inoperable
"The *blame thing* won't work!"

Interference
"Listen, Buster, *I am working this side of the street, you go and work the other side!*"

In the Final Analysis
"*Nobody really gives a dam[n]!*"

In the Middle of a Serious Conversation
"You have really nice teeth!"

Inquiring People
"*You ask me no questions, and I tell you no lies.*"

Irritation
"*You are enough to make anybody commit hari-kari!*"

Instilling
"I have to keep repeating myself to you *until I drill it into your thickhead!*"

Intelligence
"It is much better to be quiet and let people think you are intelligent than to open your mouth *and remove all doubt!*"

Jealousy
"I see *a green-eyed monster.*"

Judging Others
"But for the grace of God, *it could be you!*"

Junk
"*What's all this truck?*"

Justification to Spend Money
"Well, *you can't take it with you!*"

Keeping Order in the House
"Well, you need to *learn how to clean up after yourself!*"

Keeping Up with Housework
"Keeping up with all this stuff is *a blame nuisance*!"

Keeping Your Distance
"Some people you have to *feed with a long-handled spoon*."

Know-It-Alls
"They know everything and *been everywhere twice*."

Laggers
"They are taking their *pussy-footing* good time!"

Late Sleepers
"Get up here, child, *before the sun bakes wheat cakes in your behind*!"

Learn as Much as You Can
"Don't depend on your parents, they may not always be here, they may die!"
Note: You need to know how to be self-sufficient.

Less Fortunate
"They should be pitied more than scorn."
Note: She had been less fortunate in her youth, especially during the Great Depression.

Life
"Life can be a tough 'tiddy,' but it's got to be sucked!"
Note: She had seen hard times in her life and survived.

Listening to Lamenters
"Well, I just heard *another episode* of their story!"

Long Life
"The key to a long life is *moderation in everything*!"

Lost Friendship
"Hold on to the almighty dollar until it screams out, 'I am your friend'!"

Losing Patience
"Don't make me keep asking you to do the same thing over and over again!"

Lost Patience
"God, *help me to do right!"*

Lost Your Mind
"Have you taken leave of your *cotton-picking senses?"*

Lover and Marriage
"It all boil downs to women love money, and me love sex!"

Love Songs and Movies
"It is just *a bunch of malarkey!"*

Low Energy in Senior Years
"Getting *everything done is such an effort!"*

Lower Expectations
"If you don't expect anything, then your feelings won't be hurt!"

Mad
"Well, *I will wait until you get glad!"*

Make Up Your Mind
"Stop, pussy footing around!"

Making Sense of Saving Money
"Well, *that money will look just as nice on my bank statement,* as it would be on Mr. Man's!"

Malfunctioning Person
"They are *warped"*

Maximum Efficiency
"Kill two birds with one stone."

Maurice's Generosity
"Look, Ros [my dad], *the boy is paying off like a slot machine!"*

Meaningless Efforts
"You are not doing anything, but *an exercise in futility*!"

Men or Boys Who Think They Know Women
"You don't know a blame thing about that, *so keep your damn mouth shut*!"
Note: She did not like men in the affairs of women's domain.

Men's Dormitory Talk: Shit, Shower, and Shave in an Hour, or Cold as a Witch's Tit
"Now you don't need to repeat that!"
Note: She was humored by men's vulgarity, but didn't think it helped anything.

Men Who Need Haircut
"Hey, Ace, *you are cheating the barber*!"

Men Who Stand to Urinate
"You men aren't doing anything but hitting, missing, and pissing all around the toilet. Don't you realize women have to go in behind you, *put up the seat, and aim right*?"

Misfortune
"Well, may the saints preserve us."

Misfortune Repeatedly
"*Life is a veil of tears*!"

Missing Sugar
"Boy, are you using all of my sugar to make lemonade?"

Morbidly Obese
"I just don't see how they don't break the toilet?"
Note: Biblically, she believed morbid obesity equated with gluttony, and gluttony was a sin.

More Time Needed
"I need more time *to toss things over* in my mind!"

Most Important Thing in Life
"Learn how to take care of your own damn self, if you take care of yourself, then we wouldn't need all these social programs that we are all paying for!"

Mothers
"When your mother is gone, *everybody* is gone!"
Note: Your mother is the very last person on earth you can trust.

Mother's Pain
"I am divorced from all my children!"
Note: Disappointed with each children, all at the same time.

Move On
"Well, that's *water over the dam!"*

Narrow Escape
"But for the grace of God!"

Never Be Broke
"Always be able to put your hands on a dollar!"

Ninety-Five Years Old and Still Loves Fashion
"Oh child! I will wear something stunning!"
Note: I asked, "What are you wearing to church tomorrow?'

No Answer Available
"God only knows!"

No Engagements
"My calendar is lily white!"

No Good Man
"When you take the big cookie, *you get all the crumbs that come with it!"*

No Hope for a Person
"Oh! *They have just gone to seed!"*

No Leftover on the Dinner Plate
"Clean your plate, we don't waste food around here!"

No Money in Old Age
"I don't know why these people don't have any money in old age. *They know they are going to get old on the day they are born!"*

No Need for Further Discussion
"For all intents and purposes, the conversation is over, *why keep hashing it out!"*

No Need to Do Housework All in One Day
"Rome wasn't built in a day, do some and leave some!"

No Need to Spend Every Penny
"It [money] *will keep!"*

No Plan for Old Age
"Yeah, they were living high on the hog with big house and big car debt, *and now they are laying up in a nursing home with no money,* now what kind of sense does that make?"

No Style
"What is *all that getup* you have on?"

Nocturnal Emissions
While doing the laundry, she would yell, "'What are you doing up there boy?'"

Nonsense
"I don't want you walking around, *talking like you don't have any sense!"*

Normal
"That's just stand operating procedures!"

Not Feeling Well
"Well, I am *not feeling up to snuff* today."

Not Saving Money
"You are taking more out of the bank than you are putting in, you are saving nothing!"

Not Thinking, Kindly Speaking
"You don't have the presence of mind."

Not Thinking, Not So Gentle
"Have you taken leave from your senses?"

Nonsense Question
"You must be out of your *ever-loving* mind!"

Obsession with Neatness or Tidiness
"You are just making more work for yourself that is totally unnecessary!"

Old Age and Chronic Illness
"You might just as well be dead as to go through this!"

Old and Feeble
"Those poor old souls!"

Old and Idol
"I am a home, *just going from chair to chair!"*

Old, Cracking Bones
"Your cracking bones *sound like a crap game!"*

Old, But You Have to Keep Going
"You've got to *push yourself!"*

Old Movements
"You aren't doing nothing but just *teetering around!"*

One Bathroom for Five People
"Everybody's *bowels are coming down at the same time!"*

Oops
"Dog bit it!"

Out of Your Mind
"I know *you must be sick*!"

Overjoyed
"You look like a child on Christmas morning!"

Overly Helpful
"Now don't go and make a nuisance of yourself, you have done enough."

Overspending
"You are spending money *hand over fist*!"

Overspending of Her Money
"Child, you are taking money out of both ends of my wallet."

Pants Too Short on a Man
"Those pants are for high waters."

Par for the Course
"The situation is normal, snafu!"

Paying the Higher Price for Goods
"The quality lasts when the price is long forgotten!"

Persistently Negative People
"Some people *always have an ax to grind*!"

Person Who Tells Everything
"Telephone, telegraph, and tell . . . !"

Person Who Won't Stop Talking
"They have a *mouth almighty and tongue everlasting*!"

Picky Food Eaters
"You are eating like a bird, just *pecking at your food*!"

Placing Too Much Food on Your Plate
"Your eyes are bigger than your belly!"

Planning for the Future
"You just have to look down the road to see what is before you!"

Pleasant Conversation
"We are just sitting here, *chewing the fat*!"

Pleasant Surprise
"Well as I live and breathe!"

Poor Advice
"Don't pay that *no rabbit mind*!"

Poor Behavior
"Why are you acting so thickheaded?"

Poor Job
"Some old man that has done a half-assed job!"

Predictable
"Well, now that is a *foregone conclusion*!"

Poor Workmanship
"You can't get people to get the job done right *for love nor money*!"

Price Increases
"Stores have the prices of everything *all hiked up*!"

Priorities
"Always take care of your business first!"

Promising Money
"Now don't go out here *making promises with your mouth that your wallet can't keep*!"

Provider Husband
"You make the living, and *I will make the living worth wild*!"

Psychologically Weak Person
"You are a case!"

Puberty with Too Much Mouth
"You must be beginning to smell yourself, thinking you are grown!"

Punishing a Child
"It's harder on me, than it is on you!"

Quick to Judgement
"You run your mouth and let me run my business!"

Rainy Days
"It's good for the ducks!"

Raising Children
"It is *more than a notion* to raise a child."

Raising Children
"Children are enough to make you lose your religion!"

Ready for Bed
"I am *ready to get horizontal*!"

Regularity of Housework
"Housework is so repetitive!"

Reply When Asked "How Are You Doing Today"
"Almost!"

Revenge
"There is no need to cut off your nose to spite your face!"

Ridiculous Story
"Now here they come with some *sob story* and expecting you to feel sorry for them!"

Sameness
"I don't want a steady diet of it!"

Sated
"I am as full as a tick!"

Saving Money
"If you make a nickel, save a cent."

Seeing You in between Visits
"Okay! I see in the funny papers!"

Self-Righteous
"Never be nasty to another person *for you never know* who *you will need* to bring you a cup of water one day!"

Self-Sufficiency
"Learn to take care of yourself because your mother may not always here to care for you!"

Selfish Individuals
"It's hooray for me and to hell with everybody else!"

Seriously
"Well, I swear to my rest!"

Serving Food
"Take what you want, but eat it all!"

Shiftless Child
"Go *make yourself useful!*"

Sick for Too Long
"You can be sick, *but you had better not stay sick too long* because it's tiring working, and eventually, *nobody gives a damn.*"

Sitting around Doing Nothing
"You are *not even hitting a lick at a black snake!*"

Sleazy Person
"They have just turned to seed."

Slipups of Speech
"*There are a many of slips, between the cup and the lips!*"

Slow Movement
"You are moving *as if rigor mortis has set in!*"

Slow to Action
"Well, don't just stand there like you don't have good sense. *I expect you to move when I am talking to you.*"

Small Kitchen
"This kitchen is too small, it is just enough room to walk in and back out!"

Snack
"Well, eat a little something, *it will hold body and soul together* until dinnertime!"

Sneaky Person
"Mark my word, they have an *ulterior motive.*"

Speak Up
"Don't shake your head. Open your mouth and speak like you have good sense!"

Secrets
"If one person knows, *the whole world* knows!"

Spoiled Adult
"You are not worth a *plumb nickel*!"

Spoiled Child
"You are *spoiled rotten.*"

Stay Out of My Business
"You run your mouth and *let me run my business!*"

Staying with a Cheating Man
"Why cut your own throat? Why get a divorce when he pays the rent and doesn't abuse you? Where am I going with a high school diploma and three children?

Steady
"Well, keep a stiff upper lip!"

Still Married
"Yes! I am still serving time!"

Stomach Fat at Forty
"Child! It ain't nothing but *middle-age spread, an expanding waistline!*"

Stop Talking
"*Hush* your mouth!"

Store Coupons and Old Age
"Baby doll, honey child, Mother doesn't have time for store coupons. It is all I can do to stand up behind this cart [grocery] and put the food in it!"

Story Beautifully Told
"*You are a talking sensation!*"

Stress
"*I don't want another thing added to me!*"

Stubbornness
"You are just *hell-bent* on doing the wrong thing."

Stuck in the Workplace
"You are in a *dead-end* job."

Substitute for Profanity
"Dog bit it!"

Support Underwear Need for Men
"I just don't know why men sit with their legs spread, with all there balls hanging out and everything showing?"

Supporting a Less Confident Person
"Well, there is nothing short on you but your hair, and that's got time to grow!"

Talkative Person
"They can talk the legs off an iron kettle!"

Talking Too Long
"You are mouth almighty and tongue everlasting, don't you ever shut up?"

Tall Man
"You look like a tall glass of water."

Technological Age
"All of these companies out here, claim to have good customer, but there is no customer service because you have to do everything your dam[n] self!"

Teen Pregnancy
"Now, don't you go out here making no babies because *I am not rocking no babies.*"

Teenage Logic
"The older you get, *the dumber you get!*"

Teenagers
"You are damned if you do, and you are damned if you don't!"

Teeth
"You got a nice *set of crockery.*"

Telling All of Your Business
"Familiarity breeds contempt, *people don't wish you well!*"

Thank You
"Well, *God loves you!*"

The Know-It-All Person
"They know everything and *have been everywhere twice!*"

Tight with Money
"You must have the first dollar you ever earned!

Tired of Too Many Children Questions
"Baby doll, honey child, *Mommy doesn't know!*"

To Her Children
"You have a mother, I was motherless!"

Too Much Activity
"Hey! It's *too much commotion* in here!"

Too Much Noise
"Hey! You can stay here, but the noise has got to go!"

Too Quiet
"Well, *you don't need to sit there like a statue.*"

Tough Times
"*That's life!*"

Troubled
"Sit yourself down, *you need a little pep talk!*"

Troublesome People
"Just *stay away from them!*"

Trust Me
"I have lived long enough to see it happen!"

Trying to Get People to Do the Right Thing
"Sometimes, you can't get people to do the right thing for love nor money!"

Two Bad Options
"Well, I guess, you have to *choose between the lesser of two evils!*"

Two People Avoiding Each Other
"You all are not doing anything but *playing cat and mouse!*"

Ugly Feet
"Your feet look like the back of an alligator!"

Unbelievable
"Well, *Lordy day!*"

Unemployed
"The man is so lazy *he won't even work in a pie shop!*"

Unexpected
"Well, I swear to my rest!"

Unexpected Visitor
"Well, *another country heard from!*"

Unhappy Mood
"Well today *I am not feeling jubilant!*"

Unintelligent
"Because *you are thickheaded!*"

Unjust Accusations
"Well, *that's like the pot calling the kettle black!*"

Unkind World
"We live in a *dog-eat-dog* world."

Unnecessary Illness
"Well, ain't that *a crying shame!*"

Unpredictable
"*Invariably,* something is going to pop up that will change your plan."

Unprepared
"Don't go running out of here *all half-cocked!*"

Unreliable Worker
"They are just *fly by night!*"

Unspoken Truth
"*As quiet as it is kept*"

Unsympathetic
"*Nobody gives a damn!*"

Untimely Telephone Call
"Well, just tell them *I am in the latrine!*"

Unwanted Baby
"*Just another mouth to feed!*"

Useless
"*You are like a cow that produces a good bucket of milk, then turns around and kicks it over!*"

Value, Useless
"*You know, you are not worth a quarter!*"

Vigorous Entry
"You guys are *coming in here like gangbusters!*"

Waiting
"*Until such a time* that it comes available."

Wastefulness

"You live in waste, *you die in want!*

Watching Your Tone of Voice
"You had better cut your cards mighty close!"

Weak Justification
"Now, here you come up with *some song and dance!*"

Well Designated Tea or Coffee Cup
"Has a *lip grip.*"

What
"*In in the name of the Father*, what?"

What Choice Do I Have?
"*It is six in one hand and a half dozen in the other!*"

When a Person Entered Her House and Left the Door Open
"Hey? *Don't they have doors where you come from?*"

When Requesting Too Many Favors
"Well, *how is your blood pressure* today?"

Whippings
"Go to your room, pull off your clothes, and call me when you are ready. *If I can't talk it in your heads, I will beat it in your backsides!*"

Wild Children
"These children are *about to set me crazy!*"

Willingness
"I will, if the good Lord is willing, *and if the creeks don't rise!*"

Wishing for a Little Bit of Luck!
"Well, I hope forty cents!"

Won't Talk Too Much Today
"I am not getting *all winded up.*"

43

Word Differentiation
"I don't call you son because you shine, I call you son because you're mine!"

World News
"The world has just gone to seed!"

Worthless
"What is all this glop?"
Note: This applied to everything undesirable to her.

Wrong Doings
"Now *ain't that a sin and a shame!*"

Young Hotshots
"And now they have gotten all *old and feeble!*"

Young People
"Live your life, I have lived mine."

CHAPTER FOUR

Virtuous Woman

Who can find a virtuous woman? For
her price is far above rubies.

—*Proverbs 31:10*

With all of my mothers witticisms and adlibs, I saw her life as one of virtue. From the time she was born, it appeared from my lens on life she had come from very difficult circumstances at many levels.

After the death of her mother, my mother was forced to learn to take on most of the roles relegated to women of her era. She did all the washing, ironing, cooking, cleaning, raising her younger sister and brother, as well as attending church on Sundays and school on weekdays. She would tell stories of how unprepared she was for each of these duties and how her siblings complained of how her home management did not match her mother's. They had no idea of the work load she was undertaking, trying to run a household at such an early age. Her father knew it was hard work, but my mother said he was lazy. I couldn't believe the stories of her father making her change a tire on the car. He would sit in the window inside the house and tell her what she needed to do. I did not know him well or for very long. He passed away when I was only eight years old, but for that short period of time, I did not understand him or like him. He would also whip his children, except for the middle girl because she was frail and sickly like her mother. Under the circumstances, my mother held her own and was just grateful that he worked and paid for them all to have food, clothing, and shelter. Deep inside herself, she knew she was in a good position because she learned early that she could take care of herself if necessary.

The church setting was very much imbedded in her life. The family, initiated by her mother, insisted that the family go to church every Sunday. It was her dream before marriage to become a missionary; thus, Christianity had its roots in both families. My mother always enjoyed the relief of getting out of the house on Sunday for a few hours; it was some relief from her responsibilities after combing and brushing hair and ironing clothes for her sibling so that they would look presentable at church. She enjoyed and memorized the words of the hymns. Her Christianity carried her throughout her entire life.

When she married my father, she was required to convert to Catholicism and raise any children of the marriage Catholic. She did not like Catholic Church services at all, since the mass was spoken in Latin, and she did not understand a word of what was being said. There was also no choir to sing African American Methodist hymns. Just as soon as I turned eighteen, she went back to the Methodist Church that she was familiar, and she worked very hard and made her tithes each month. My mother did not come from a wealthy background, but she was compassionate to the poor and was extremely generous to the less fortunate, especially children. She carried her childhood memories, and they influenced her giving. In her last will and testament, she left money to the Feed the Children charity. My mother had known hunger during the Great Depression, thus could identify with the charity.

My mother was a good wife, and my father was a great husband, but as in most marriages, they experienced their ups and downs. They, from my observation, were not always pretty. They were a great team when raising their three children. My dad was kind, but he also possessed a militaristic style and staunchness, as he had learned in Catholic school; thus, he required obedience with almost every breath we took as children. My mother, of course, had her aphorisms as backup!

My mother washed, ironed, cooked, and cleaned for my dad and took great pride in ironing his starched shirts. She even ironed his underwear. Ironing was her favorite of all household chores. When my dad had his first and second heart attacks, it was my mother who nursed him back to health until she began to fail in the process. Whatever slights that transpired over their sixty-two years of marriage must have always been forgiven or resolved, for their burial marker reads Forever Together.

After I entered first grade, my mother took a job out of the home with the federal government. In addition to beautifying our home, she purchased the food and purchased all the children's clothes. She contributed significantly to our higher education. In my case, she footed the entire cost for my tuition and room and board for undergraduate school. As children, we had the biggest Christmas, Easter, birthday, and back-to-school clothes among most of the children in our community. We wanted for nothing.

For a brief period of time, she also took in her sister's child for 6–12 months. The child appeared to like my mother more than his own.

During her thirty-year career and her life as a Negro woman, she faced many disheartening issues of social injustice. After completing her thirty years of service and never missing a day of work for the last ten years of her employment, she was denied entry to the restaurant where the party her colleagues were hosting for her outstanding performance was being held. My mother was not hurt; *she kept a stiff upper lip*!

I would describe my mother as a virtuous daughter, Christian, wife, mother, and colleague. She was strong and a survivor in an often inhospitable world.

CHAPTER FIVE

Looking Back, an Article

*Give her of the fruit of her hands; and let
her own works praise her in the gates.*

Proverbs 31:31

When my mother was seventy-eight years old, she wrote an article entitled "Looking Back." She described the early years of her marriage; being married; World War II era; Edgewood, Maryland, where we lived; and military property Edgewood Arsenal, where my dad was stationed. She wrote,

> During the years of the 2nd World War 1941–1945, housing was at a premium for African Americans. People had come from many, many states across the country searching for war work. In Edgewood, Maryland, the setting for this paper, the U.S. Government leased a parcel of land to build projects. These projects would house civilians engaged in war work and their military families.
>
> The projects were divided by on main road, namely, Tremble Road. White residences lived on one side of the road and African Americans on the other. For this paper, we will be addressing the side where the colored people lived (that is what we were called then).

This area consisted of four streets, namely: Battle, Hartman, Cull and Wilson.

The dwellings were one story houses composed of cement blocks, and two story one and two-bedroom apartments finished in shingle.

Whether you were an officer, enlisted man or civilian, we all lived there together.

There was one telephone booth in the area for making calls. No one had private phones during those years.

There was a building that housed a rental office, staffed by Mr. Jerome Jones and his secretary. The building encompassed a recreation hall, where children played games during the day. On weekends, dances were held for adults, with music provided by local bands or "juke boxes" wailing to the Mills Brothers, "Till Then", Ella Fitzgerald's "Sunny Side of the Street", Dinah Washington's "This Bitter Earth", the Ink Spots, Nat King Cole, Lionel Hampton, Count Basie and others.

Also, in the building was a nursery, for working parents sponsored by the Bel Air Board of Education. The teachers were M's Linton and M's Warren. Zelma Dorsey assisted the teachers and prepared the children's lunches.

We had one available doctor whose name I do not recall now but later followed Dr. Stewart and Dr. Kahan.

The two grocery stores were ½ mile away, Schmick's and Perry's. One would walk down the road to buy their groceries and hire Crawford's cab to return.

Remember the variety store and pin-ball machine arcade?

Our three maintenance men were Mr. Sam Jones, Mr.

Webster and Mr. Williams who kept our area clean. They would ride around on motor bikes as they fired the furnaces for the apartments and checked on security. Those in the block houses fired their own pot-belly stoves. Mr. Bailey was the ice man.

Few people locked doors, no safety doors, no drive-by shootings. Everyone was congenial.

For a long time, Mr. James Spriggs, Sr. had the only car in the development. (During the war years, no automobiles were made, all factories had been retooled for war machinery. Mr. Spriggs would transport the girls to the Edgewood or Aberdeen Post to dance to the Army's outstanding 327 Band—Remember Sgts. Curtis, Will, Duck, Kearsey, et al.?).

Of course, since we were only half mile from the Army Post, that the Pennsylvania Railroad serviced, we would ride the 10:06 A.M. train to Baltimore (or for that matter anywhere) and the 10:50 P.M. train back. For a more frequent schedule you had to depend on an old "beat-up" Dependable Motor Tours Bus. We would ride this to Baltimore for clothes, furniture, and a wider selection of food from Schreiber's, or the Lexington Markets. Because of shortages in everything we had government issued ration books (especially for meats). Sometimes siren would sound for "black-outs" all lights would go out and we would cover our windows for fear enemy planes would fly over and see the lights and bomb us. Fire warden would patrol the streets.

But! We were young, innocent and were hardly cognizant of the world around us. We danced, drank whiskey, beautified our humble dwellings, played cards, loved, married and had our babies! I remember-

It was hot one summer night, we were sound asleep at

11:30 P.M., Mr. Spriggs had an amazing sense of humor. He walked up to the bedroom window, removed the screen and hollered in—"Get-Up", we are getting together a bid-whisk card game.

We had great fun. We knew there was a war "over there", but we were not knowledgeable of the casualties, except for those who worked at Perry Point Veterans Hospital. They nursed the wounded as they returned from overseas.

We laughed, played, joked, and had wonderful times. We also worked hard. Many of the neighbors swung shifts around the clock 8 to 4, 4 to 12 and 12 to 8.

1945, we rejoiced the war was over, with victory for the allied forces. Our husbands, son, and father were coming home (WAC's too!)

We began to settle down, the realization of life started to register. We had to think of the future, we had to raise our children, cloth, feed and look forward to educating them. With the war over industry was turning out new appliances, we struggled to obtain electric refrigerators, automatic washers, automobiles, televisions, new homes, etc.

The "passion pits—the mad love."

Well! Well!

So, here we are—Lets look back, pray for, and remember, so many that were among us, who have passed on- and also those who could not be here with us today. Death gives us a sense of our own mortality.

A philosopher once said: "It was a shame that youth was wasted on the young", meaning, of course, if we only had the wisdom when we were young, we know now, but too old to use.

I wager there would be but a few, that would want to return to what we then thought of as fun times, "A Ball"!

Remember Shakespeare's seven soliloquies of life? "San's everything."

Let's thank God for the good time and happy moments we have shared together-but pray for love and peace in the world for a better tomorrow for those who will follow us.

Submitted by Zelma V. Dorsey

September 15, 1997

EPILOGUE

In the final analysis, the United States of America has changed somewhat since the birth and life of my mother.

The two world wars have ended, but global dissention remains a persistent issue.

President Wilson maintained segregation.

The United States Armed Forces were integrated under the Truman Administration. Schools and housing were also integrated in the Truman Administration.

Women can now vote; there seems to be a roll back on women's rights.

Race is a perpetual issue, and like women's rights, racial concern remains prevalent, and it appears to be rolling backward.

Riots and protests are in much larger numbers and seem to be the only way for popular opinion to be expressed.

Communism is still a threat, as it has always been.

Voter suppression is at an all-time high.

In my mother's family, her mother died when she was eight years old. Her father died on Labor Day in 1955. Her brother died, and Agnes lives on to this day at 102 years old.

She raised her children, providing them with health, strength, and a chance to make it.

She worked for the United States Department of Defense at Edgewood Arsenal for thirty years, never missing a day for illness in the last ten years that she worked. Her income, along with my dad's income, brought them into the solid range of the middle class, which had been a dream for both of them.

She procured all the material possessions she desired. She was married for sixty-two years. Her husband passed away. She lived an additional fifteen years and had the opportunity to recover as a single lady, lost as a child. She shopped until she almost dropped.

She passed away at age ninety-five, leaving something to each family member and to the Feed the Children charity.

My mother continues to talk to me each day and lives in every single minute of every day in me.

She would always say, regardless of my choices, "You are my child." Even when I disappointed her. My mother's final address was my address in Washington, DC, her hometown.

My mother was blessed, and I was blessed by her wisdom. She said she had a happy life when all was said and done.

BIBLIOGRAPHY

Birth Certificate, Zelma Virginia Curry, District of Columbia, September 2, 1919.

Death Notice, the Staunton New-Leader, Wednesday, November 16, 1927.

Marriage License, State of Maryland, November 17, 1939.

Certificate of Baptism, St. Pius, Baltimore, Maryland, March 26, 1942.

Letter, Office of Board of Education of Harford County, Maryland, October 9, 1944.

Army of the United States, Honorable Discharge, William H. Curry Jr., January 6, 1946.

Letter, Magnolia School, Magnolia, Maryland, January 23, 1948.

Personnel Action, United States Army, July 26, 1948.

Personal History Statement, United States Government, DC, February 15, 1951.

United States Civil Service Commission, Notice of Rating, October 19, 1951.

United States Civil Service Commission, Notice of Rating, January 17, 1952.

Veteran Administration Hospital, Perry Point, Maryland, January 2, 1953.

Public Housing Administration, Washington, DC, September 24, 1954.

Department of the Army, Notice of Personnel Action, January 20, 1955.

Death Certificate, William H. Curry Sr., District of Columbia, September 5, 1955.

Last Will and Testament of William H. Curry, Washington, DC, May 12, 1955.

United States District Court, Holding in Probate Court, Washington, DC, May 12, 1955.

Death Certificate, William H. Curry Sr., District of Columbia, September 2, 1955.

Education Resume, February 17, 1960.

Chemical Corp Civilian Personnel Management Inventory, September 14, 1960.

Housing and Billeting Office, Army Chemical Center, September 20, 1960.

Department of the Army Certificate of Ten Years of Service, September 30, 1963.

Qualifications Inventory, Librarianship, October 18, 1961.

Letter, Orders, Temporary Duty, United States Army, Edgewood Arsenal, April 1, 1966.

Letter, Public Schools of the District of Columbia, Washington, DC, June 21, 1968.

Worksheet for National Agency Check Request, Edgewood Arsenal, Maryland, July 9, 1969.

Notice of Personnel Action, Mass Change, Edgewood Arsenal, Maryland, June 21, 1971.

Certificate of Membership, Ames United Methodist Church, July 18, 1971.

Harford Community College, General Studies, June, 1971.

United States Army Certificate of Recognition, Accumulated Leave, April 1, 1976.

Department of the Army, Outstanding Performance, September 12, 1977.

The Ryrie Study Bible, King James Version, Moody Press, Chicago, 1978.

Department of the Army, Letter of Commendation, October 30, 1978.

Receipt, Becker & Becker Furriers, Philadelphia, Pennsylvania, January 27, 1979.

The Freya Club, Miss Oprah Winfrey, Aberdeen, Maryland, June 17, 1979.

Notice of Personnel Action, Change in Job Number, November 1, 1979.

Notice of Personnel Action, NTE, Temporary Appointment, March 3, 1980.

Letter, Atlantic Federal Savings and Loan Association, House Deed, June 3, 1980.

Department of State, Passport Application, September 28, 1981.

Time line of African American History, 1901–1925, Johnson Publishing Company, Chicago, 1982.

Receipt, Mano Swartz Furriers, September 25, 1987.

Letter, Georgetown University Hospital, RE: William H. Curry Jr., March 3, 1988.

Letters from Japan, from Maurice S. Dorsey and Deloris Austin Dorsey, November 24, 1990–July 16, 1991.

Lease Agreement, Home Properties, Owings Run Apartments, May 1, 1999.

Lengold Realty, Inc., Offered for Sale, 1908 Lincoln Road, July, 1999.

Metzger's Auction Service, Household Inventory, July 8, 1999.

Death Certificate, James Roswell Dorsey Sr., December 2, 2000.

Harford County Maryland, Office of County Executive, Certificate of Appreciation, Zelma Dorsey, April 28, 2001.

Wall of Tolerance, National Campaign for Tolerance, Zelma V. Dorsey, signed by Morris Dees, Co-Chair, and Rosa Parks, Co-Chair, February 17, 2003.

Death Certificate, William H. Curry Jr., June 16, 2004.

Letter of Lease Termination, Maurice W. Dorsey, PhD, July 11, 2005.

Death Certificate, Zelma Virginia Dorsey, September 27, 2014.

1919, *The Year That Changed America*, Martin W. Sandler, 2019

Of Time and Spirit, Maurice W. Dorsey, September, 2020.

ALSO BY THE AUTHOR

Of Time and Spirit: A Tribute to My Father—a father's journey to inner peace and his struggles learning to communicate with his son (2020)

From Whence We Come—a family saga and the struggles of a child coming to terms with being gay and Black in a Christian family (2017)

Businessman First: Remembering Henry G. Parks, Jr. 1916–1989 Capturing the Life of a Businessman Who Was African American A Biography (2014)

Awards

2021 Independent Book Award Distinguished Favorite: *Of Time and Spirit* (2020); *From Whence We Come* (2017); and *Businessman First: Remembering Henry G. Parks, Jr. 1916–1989 Capturing the Life of a Businessman Who Was African American, A Biography* (2014).

2015 QBR Phillis Wheatley Book Award, Finalist, *Businessman First: Remembering Henry G. Parks, Jr. 1916–1989 Capturing the Life of a Businessman Who Was African American, A Biography.*

Article

Alpha Kappa Alpha Sorority, Inc., Issuu.com, June 26, 2021.

Podcasts

The Black Male Archives, Interview via YouTube, July 8, 2022.

Conquering Everest Podcast, August 7, 2021.

Blackopolypse Podcast Media, Amsterdam, Berlin, Rome, Stockholm, Vienna, July 5, 2021.

Queer Voicez Podcast, May 17, 2021.

Blackopolypse Podcast Media, Amsterdam, Berlin, Rome, Stockholm, Vienna, April 27, 2021.

Gays Over 40 Podcast, February 27, 2021.

Bathrobe Moments Podcast, February 12, 2021

Lectures

Baltimore Office on Aging, Senior Box Office, April 12, 2022.

University of Maryland–College Park, Across Generations, Black Terp Existence at the UMD, a Panel Presentation and Online via Zoom, April 7, 2022.

Washington Culinary Historians of Washington, DC, Virtual Presentation, January 9, 2022.

University of Maryland-College Park, Reparative Histories Oral History Project, December 16, 2021.

The Life of a Businessman Who Was African American, A Biography, November 9, 2021.

Association for the Study of African American Life and History, a Negro Military Family at Edgewood Arsenal, Maryland, Virtual Presentation, September 23, 2021.

University of Maryland, Doctoral Career Pathways Virtual Conference, April 30, 2021.

University of Maryland Career Days Virtual Panel Discussion, January 27, 2021.

Others
Donation and Interview with Baltimore Museum of Industry, May 24, 2022.

Wikipedia Draft Entry for Henry G. Parks Jr., March 1, 2022.

INDEX

Forty-Ninth Street NE, 7

G

German shepherd, 6
Great Depression, 6–7, 46
grocery stores, 49

I

ironing, 46

J

Jones, Jerome, 49

L

laws, child labor, 6
Lewis, Robert, 7
life, 45, 47, 51, 54, 60–62
"Looking Back" (Curry-Dorsey), 48
Lucretia Mott Elementary School, 7

M

Mae. *See* Curry, Mary Letcher
maintenance men, 49
marriage, xiii, 4, 7, 28, 46–47
Marshall, Thurgood, 2
Masonic meetings, 6
Methodist Church, 46

N

National Association for the Advancement of Colored People (NAACP), 2
Negro family, 4, 7
Northeast Washington, 7
nursery, 49

P

Peacock (black man), 5
Perry Point Veterans Hospital, 51

projects, 48

R

race, 53
race riots, 1–2, 53
ration books, 50
recreation hall, 49
responsibilities, adult, xi
rights
African American, 1
of women, 53
Roosevelt, Theodore, 1

S

social injustice, 47
Souls of Black Folk, The (Du Bois), 1
Spriggs, James, Sr., 50–51
success, 5, 8

T

teachers, 49
1007 Monroe Street NW, 7
327 Band, 50
Tremble Road, 48
Truman Administration, 53

U

United States Armed Forces, 53
United States Department of Defense, 53
United States of America, 2, 53

V

voter suppression, 53

W

wars, 51, 53
Washington, Booker T., 1
White House, 1
White House cook, 2

white men, 5
Willie (aunt), 7
Wilson, Woodrow, 2
wisdom, 3, 51, 54
Woodrow, Wilson, 2, 53
World War I, 2

Z

Zelma's Aphorisms, Old-School Wisdom, Instructive, Inspirational, Hilarious to Outrageous (Maurice), xi, 2, 4

CPSIA information can be obtained
at www.ICGtesting.com
Printed in the USA
LVHW042231291022
731895LV00002B/131